CHECKING

ON THE

BOAT

MYSTIC SEAPORT®

HENRY HOLT AND COMPANY
NEW YORK

A SCOTCH BONNET PRESS BOOK

Acknowledgments

To Chris Cox, for the exhortations
To Dan Benfield, for the explanations

Henry Holt and Company, Inc.
Publishers since 1866
115 West 18th Street
New York, New York 10011

Henry Holt ® is a registered trademark of Henry Holt and Company, Inc.

Published in Canada by Fitzhenry & Whiteside Ltd.,
195 Allstate Parkway, Markham, Ontario L3R 4T8

Library of Congress Cataloging-in-Publication Data available on request.

ISBN 0-8050-5469-3
Henry Holt books are available for special promotions and premiums.
For details contact: Director, Special Markets.
First Edition: 1997

A SCOTCH BONNET PRESS BOOK, MYSTIC, CT 06355
Designed, developed and produced by Nan Jernigan and Louise Desjardins

PRINTED IN ITALY
All first editions are printed on acid-free paper.

1   3   5   7   9   10   8   6   4   2

*C*hecking on the Boat will help you to organize important details about your boat, record memories of significant experiences and sights on the water, and store photographs of your boat in one central location. Beginning with the purchase of the boat, writing entries a few lines at a time will create a journal that will help you remember the highlights of your time spent on your boat.

A major aspect of boat ownership is the maintenance of the boat. Use this book as a record of essential information about your boat and its equipment. The Equipment on Board list is a place to create a permanent record of serial number and warranty information. The Boat Specification and Supplier lists help you keep track of the items you will want to look for on your next trip to a marine supply store. Keep *Checking on the Boat* on board, and you can write down items as you think of them. This book will help you to organize your thoughts and tasks when you are on land or on the water.

Also, use the book to record the best parts of boat ownership—cruising, fishing, and the overall enjoyment of being on the water. Great storms, the time you misjudged the tide and it added four hours to your trip, a moonlit night with a lighthouse on the horizon, a fabulous restaurant you found in a small harbor town—all of these events can be recorded and can become part of your personal history of the time spent on your boat. The photos in the book are from the world renowned collection of Mystic Seaport. Add your own photos to these pages to create your personal collection of boating memories.

Contents

Boat Information

Vessel name _____

License number _____

VHF Radio information (Call letters) _____

Type of vessel _____

Home port _____

Registration number _____

Owner's name _____

Address _____

Telephone _____

Choosing the Boat

I first began to look for a boat _____

I found my boat _____
                    BOATING MAGAZINES, WANT ADS, BOAT YARD, FRIEND

_____

My family's choice for a boat was _____

_____

The boat we chose was _____

_____

and we chose this style and model of the boat because _____

_____
              CRUISING DISTANCE, CABIN STYLE, SPEED

_____

_____

_____

_____

What the boat looked like the day I bought it.

History of the Boat

The boat was manufactured by _____

_____

_____

and it was designed by _____

The boat was built in _____

The previous owners of the boat were _____

_____

and they harbored the boat in _____

_____

A few interesting yarns about the boat are _____

_____

STORMS WEATHERED, BIG FISH CAUGHT, RACES WON

_____

_____

"A Comfortable Boat"
Four things shalt thou not see aboard a yacht
for its comfort—a cow, a wheelbarrow,
an umbrella and a naval officer.

Boat Specifications

Length overall _____   Length on the water line _____

Beam _____   Draft _____

Mast height above water _____

Ballast displacement _____

Hull material _____

Hull design _____
DEEP V, MODIFIED DEEP V, TRI-HULL

Boat layout _____
RUNABOUTS, BOWRIDER, CENTER CONSOLE

Cabin design _____
CUDDY CABIN, CRUISER

Engine arrangement and horsepower _____
OUTBOARD, INBOARD, STERNDRIVE, JETDRIVE

Colors _____   Number of passengers _____

Water capacity _____   Weight _____

Boat Specifications and Suppliers

Engine builder _____

Engine serial number _____ Oil capacity _____

Fuel type _____ Fuel capacity _____

Oil fuel mixture ratio _____ Fuel consumption _____

Spark plugs _____ Gap _____

Fan belt _____ Filters _____

Water pump impeller _____

Propeller diameter and pitch _____

Miscellaneous gaskets _____

Sail Boat Specifications

Auxiliary power _____

Main sail _____

Genoa sail _____

Jib sail _____

Spinnaker _____

Halyards _____
LENGTH, DIAMETER, CONSTRUCTION

Best speed under sail _____

Naming the Boat

The boat is named _____

Other names we considered were _____

_____

_____

and this name was chosen by _____

_____

_____

_____

_____

_____

_____

_____

The story behind the name choice is _____

_____

_____

_____

We christened the boat on _____

and _____

_____

_____ helped us to celebrate.

Place a photo of the boat with its name here.

Equipment on Board

16

Equipment to Purchase

_____

_____

_____

_____

_____

_____

_____

_____

_____

_____

_____

_____

_____

Bottom Paint and other Necessities

Bottom paint _____

_____

_____

ABLATIVE, EPOXY-BASED, VINYL-BASED

_____

Varnish _____

_____

Batteries _____

_____

Clamps _____

_____

Hoses _____

_____

Engine belts _____

_____

Cotter pins, cam cleats, turnbuckles _____

_____

Miscellaneous rivets and screws _____

_____

Other items _____

_____

_____

_____

Upgrades & Repairs

Engine _____
DATE COMPLETED AND WORK THAT WAS DONE

_____

_____

Hull _____

_____

_____

Cabin _____

_____

_____

_____

Navigation systems _____

_____

_____

Anchor & windlass _____

_____

Mast _____

_____

Sails _____

_____

Winches _____

_____

Sheets _____

_____

Miscellaneous _____

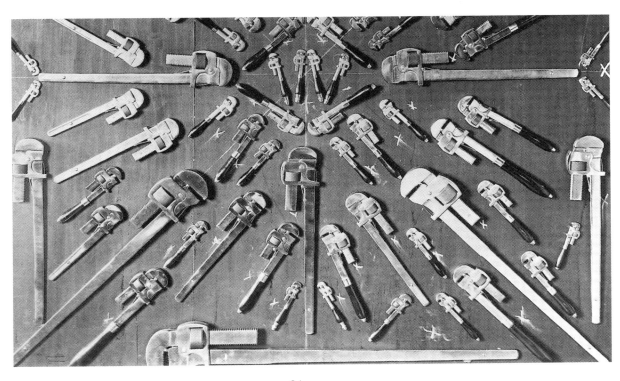

Navigational Instruments

Pedestal compass _____
MAKE, MODEL NUMBER, AND DATE OF INSTALLATION

Bulkhead compass _____

Digital magnetic compass _____

Fluxgate compass _____

Compass maintenance and interference check _____
WRITE DATES HERE

Binoculars _____
FOR HELMSMAN'S USE ONLY!

Sextant _____

Global positioning system (GPS) _____

Sat-Nav system _____

Radar set _____

VHF radio _____
RADIO OPERATOR'S LICENSE NUMBER

Handheld VHF radio _____

Ham or single sideband radio _____

Automatic pilot _____

Depth sounder _____

Speedometer _____

Dividers _____

Parallel rule _____

Protractor _____

Charts _____

_____

_____

_____

Safety at Sea

Rules of the Road

The Rules of the Road are a set of regulations which apply to all vessels on inner coastal and inland waters of the United States. A skipper should be familiar with all of the Rules of the Road. The rules are available from the Government Printing Office, Washington, D.C., 20402, your local US Coast Guard districts, and authorized chart suppliers.

Right of Way Rankings: Vessels not under command
Vessels restricted in ability to manuever
Vessels engaged in fishing
Sailing vessels
Power driven vessels

Vessels must give way to vessels ranked above them. A sailboat under power is considered a power vessel even if its sails are up.

"Ships Passing in the Night"

Meeting steamers do not dread.
When you see three lights ahead,
Starboard wheel and show your red.

Green to green, or red to red,
Perfect safety go ahead.

If to starboard red appear,
'tis your duty to keep clear;
Act as judgment says is proper:
Port—or starboard—back or stop her.

But when upon your post is seen
A steamer starboard light of green,
There's not so much for you to do,
For green to port keeps clear of you.

Both in safety and in doubt
Always keep a good look-out;
In danger with no room to run,
Ease her—Stop her—Go astern.

Father Neptune has no patience
with those who do not respect him.

L. Francis Herreshoff
The Compleat Cruiser

A checklist of safety items to keep on board

☐ Personal flotation devices (PFD) for crew and guests
(Coast Guard approved type I, II, or III)
☐ Foul weather gear for crew and guests
☐ Man-overboard drill (Practiced in fair weather)
☐ Man-overboard gear
☐ Horseshoe ring   ☐ Life sling (Victim retrieval system)
☐ Pole   ☐ M.O.M. pack (Overboard survival pack)
☐ Strobe   ☐ Type IV throwable

☐ Signals
　　☐ Automatic lantern   ☐ Orange distress flag
　　☐ Bell   ☐ Searchlight
　　☐ Flares (Note date)   ☐ Strobelight
　　☐ Flashlight & batteries   ☐ Whistle
　　☐ Horn & extra air canisters ☐ White flag
　　☐ Megaphone & batteries

☐ EPIRB (Register with Coast Guard)

☐ Fire extinguisher (Note date)

☐ First aid kit

☐ Emergency rations

☐ Safety harness

☐ Life raft (Inspect on an annual basis)

☐ First aid kit

☐ Tool kit

☐ Tow rope

Cabin Layout

When needed, important items are stored here, in the cabin of the boat.

1. Fire extinguisher
2. Flotation devices
3. Flares/Horn
4. Bilge pump

5. First aid kit
6. Flashlights
7. Charts
8. Toolbox

*Place a drawing of your cabin layout here, and using the number system
above, indicate where each of the items is located.*

Home Port

The boat is moored at _____

_____

_____

The boat went into the water in

_____

_____

_____

and will come out of the water in

_____

_____

_____

_____

"Launching"
Frae rocks and sands
An' barren lands,
An' ill men's hands,
Keep's free.
Weel oot, weel in
Wi a guid shot.

Scottish Launch Chant

Expenditures
(How much does it really cost?)

Expenditure	Date	Cost
STORAGE FEES		
MOORING FEES/DOCKAGE FEES		

Fuel Log

Record here where you purchased fuel, the date, the cost per gallon, the total gallons and the cost per hour of fuel the engine is consuming. Also keep track of when and how much motor oil the engine is burning.

Date	Where purchased	Cost per gal.	# of gals.	Cost of Gals. p/h	Oil added

Cruising Maintenance Log

- [ ] Check blower in engine compartment
- [ ] Check bilge for fuel fumes and water levels
- [ ] Inspect and clean engine filters
- [ ] Check engine oil and water levels
- [ ] Check battery water levels
- [ ] Check VHF, GPS, electronic gear
- [ ] Check navigation lights
- [ ] Check fuel
- [ ] Top off water tanks
- [ ] Clean the head compartment

Sailboat Maintenance

- [ ] Check sails for loose stitching, rips or tears
- [ ] Check sheets and halyards for chafe and wear
- [ ] Inspect stanchion bases for missing screws and looseness
- [ ] Inspect lifelines for weak points

Cruising Checklist

- ☐ Beverages
- ☐ Books
- ☐ Charts of area
- ☐ Compass
- ☐ Engine spare parts
- ☐ Extra fuses and bulbs
- ☐ Extra hats
- ☐ Fire extinguisher
- ☐ First aid kit
- ☐ Flashlight and extra batteries
- ☐ Float plan filed
- ☐ Food checklist
- ☐ Foul weather gear
- ☐ Flotation cushions
- ☐ Ice

- ☐ Navigator's tool kit
- ☐ Passports
- ☐ Plastic bags
- ☐ Playing cards
- ☐ Signal flares
- ☐ Safety harness
- ☐ Softwood plugs
- ☐ Sun screen
- ☐ Tarpaulin
- ☐ Tools
- ☐ Waterproof chart tube

Cruising Log

Date _____

Destination _____

Point of departure _____

Time _____

Arrival point _____

Time _____

Forecast _____

Weather _____

Wind _____

Visibility _____

Sea condition _____

_____

Skipper _____

Course _____

_____

Average speed _____

Crew and guests _____

_____

Occasion for the cruise _____

Favorite sights _____

_____

Side trips on the cruise _____

_____

Successful menus and memorable restaurants _____

_____

A favorite moment on the cruise.

One hand for yourself, one hand
for the ship.

Sailor's maxim

Cruising Log

Date _____

Destination _____

Point of departure _____

Time _____

Arrival point _____

Time _____

Forecast _____

Weather _____

Wind _____

Visibility _____

Sea condition _____

_____

Skipper _____

Course _____

_____

Average speed _____

Crew and guests _____

_____

Occasion for the cruise _____

Favorite sights _____

_____

Side trips on the cruise _____

_____

Successful menus and memorable restaurants _____

_____

Cruising Log

Date _____

Destination _____

Point of departure _____

Time _____

Arrival point _____

Time _____

Forecast _____

Weather _____

Wind _____

Visibility _____

Sea condition _____

_____

Skipper _____

Course _____

_____

Average speed _____

Crew and guests _____

_____

Occasion for the cruise _____

Favorite sights _____

_____

Side trips on the cruise _____

_____

Successful menus and memorable restaurants _____

_____

In a puff, spring a luff
In a lull, keep her full.

Cruising Log

Date _____

Destination _____

Point of departure _____

Time _____

Arrival point _____

Time _____

Forecast _____

Weather _____

Wind _____

Visibility _____

Sea condition _____

_____

Skipper _____

Course _____

_____

Average speed _____

Crew and guests _____

_____

Occasion for the cruise _____

Favorite sights _____

_____

Side trips on the cruise _____

_____

Successful menus and memorable restaurants _____

_____

Cruising Log

Date _____

Destination _____

Point of departure _____

Time _____

Arrival point _____

Time _____

Forecast _____

Weather _____

Wind _____

Visibility _____

Sea condition _____

_____

Skipper _____

Course _____

_____

Average speed _____

Crew and guests _____

_____

Occasion for the cruise _____

Favorite sights _____

_____

Side trips on the cruise _____

_____

Successful menus and memorable restaurants _____

_____

Bow: The front of the boat.
Aft: The part behind the front.
Stern: The fat part behind the aft.
Wake: The water behind the part behind the aft.
Up forward: Any part of the ship in front of the stern.
Amidships: The section of the ship in front of the stern and right behind the bow.
Down below: The stuff directly beneath any of these parts.

Larence Lariar *Nautical Dictionary*

Cruising Log

Date _____

Destination _____

Point of departure _____

Time _____

Arrival point _____

Time _____

Forecast _____

Weather _____

Wind _____

Visibility _____

Sea condition _____

_____

Skipper _____

Course _____

_____

Average speed _____

Crew and guests _____

_____

Occasion for the cruise _____

Favorite sights _____

_____

Side trips on the cruise _____

_____

Successful menus and memorable restaurants _____

_____

Cruising Log

Date _____

Destination _____

Point of departure _____

Time _____

Arrival point _____

Time _____

Forecast _____

Weather _____

Wind _____

Visibility _____

Sea condition _____

_____

Skipper _____

Course _____

_____

Average speed _____

Crew and guests _____

_____

Occasion for the cruise _____

Favorite sights _____

_____

Side trips on the cruise _____

_____

Successful menus and memorable restaurants _____

_____

Evening gray and morning red
Shorten all spare sails ahead;
Evening red and morning gray
You're sure to have a fishing day.

Fishing

Favorite spots _____

_____

_____

_____

_____

_____

_____

_____

_____

"Fisherman's Hymn"
The osprey sails above the sound,
The geese are gone, the gulls are flying;
The herring shoals swarm thick around,
The nets are launched, the boats are plying.
Yo, ho, my hearts! Let's seek the deep,
Raise high the song, and cheerly wish her,
Still as at the bending net we sweep,
God bless the fish-hawk, and the fisher!

Record catches _____

_____

_____

_____

_____

_____

_____

_____

_____

_____

_____

_____

_____

_____

_____

Let me snuff thee up, sea breeze! and whinny in thy spray.

Herman Melville
White Jacket

Weather

Barometer _____
MAKE, MODEL NUMBER

_____

- A falling barometer with winds out of the east generally means bad weather.
- A rising barometer with winds shifted to the west forecasts clearing.
- When the pressure decreases at an increasing rate, a serious storm is brewing.

Anemometer _____
MAKE, MODEL NUMBER

_____

Sling psychrometer _____
MAKE, MODEL NUMBER

_____

_____

Thermometer _____
MAKE, MODEL NUMBER

_____

Apparent wind indicator _____
MAKE, MODEL NUMBER

_____

When the wind backs and the weather glass falls,
Then be on your guard against gales and squalls.

Red sky in the morning
Is a Sailor's sure warning;
Red sky at night
Is a Sailor's delight.

Foul weather gear _____

With rising wind and falling glass,
soundly sleeps the silly ass.

_____

_____

_____

First rise after low,
foretells stronger blow.

The sharper the blast,
The sooner it's past.

Cirrus clouds: *Curl clouds, mares' tails, goat hair*
Mares' tails,
Leave short sails.
Forecast: Good weather, perhaps the approach of a warm front.

Cirrostratus:
If clouds look as if scratched by a hen,
Get ready to reef your topsails then.
Forecast: Approaching wet weather.

Cirrocumulus: *Mackerel sky*
Mackerel sky, mackerel sky,
Never long wet and never long dry.
Forecast: Changeable weather.

Cumulus: *Rain balls, wool pack*
A round-topped cloud, with flattened base,
Carries rainfall in its face.

When mountains and cliffs in the clouds appear,
Some sudden and violent showers are near.

Stratus:
When mist comes from the hill, Then the weather it doth spill;
When the mist comes from the sea, Then good weather will it be.

"Little Exercises"
Think of the storm roaming
the sky uneasily like a dog
looking for a place to sleep in,
listen to it growling.

Elizabeth Bishop

Great Storms

Storms we weathered cruising_____

_____

_____

_____

_____

_____

_____

_____

_____

_____

"Sea-Chill"

I must go down to the seas again, the sport of wind and tide,
As the gray wave and the green wave play leapfrog over the side.
And all I want is a glassy calm with a bone-dry scupper,
A good book and warm rug and light, plain supper.

Arthur Guiterman

50

Weather Advisories

The National Weather Service broadcasts on VHF Channels WX-1 (162.550 MHz), WX-2 (162.400 MHz) and WX-3 (162.475 MHz). Small dedicated weather radios are also useful. The forecasts are taped broadcasts and are reissued every four hours. Listen for the marine forecast for your area as well as for the temperature, wind, and sea state conditions. Special advisories are always accompanied by visual signals displayed at Coast Guard stations, marinas, and yacht clubs.

Small craft advisory
Day: One red pennant
Night: Red light above a white light
Weather: Winds to 33 knots; means sea conditions dangerous for small craft

Gale warning
Day: Two red pennants
Night: White light above a red light
Weather: Winds to 47 knots and above; a full gale warning means winds could reach 48-63 knots if the storm is associated with a hurricane

Hurricane warning
Day: Two square red flags with black centers
Night: White light between two red lights
Weather: Winds 64 knots and above

Lighthouses

_____

_____

_____

_____

_____

A favorite lighthouse.

_____

_____

_____

_____

_____

_____

_____

_____

_____

FOG

Sea smoke:
Occurs when the water is warmer than the air flowing on top of the water

Precipitation Fog:
Occurs when a warm rain falls through a surface layer of cold air

Radiation Fog:
Forms on calm, clear nights when the earth radiates heat into cooler air

Advection Fog:
Forms when warm damp air flows over a cooler body of water

Rainbow to windward, foul fall the day,
Rainbow to leeward, rain runs away.

A backward wind says storms are nigh,
Veering winds will clear the sky.

Best Bathing Spots

_____

_____

_____

_____

_____

_____

_____

_____

_____

_____

_____

_____

_____

_____

_____

Favorite Gunkholing Adventures

_____

_____

_____

_____

_____

_____

_____

_____

_____

_____

_____

Best Harbors

Rum Punch Recipe
One of sour, two of sweet, three
of strong, and four of weak.
Lime is sour, sugar is sweet,
rum is strong, and gin is weak.

_____

_____

_____

_____

_____

_____

_____

_____

Games Afloat

Whittling

For whittling, cedar, soft pine or white wood work best. Prepare a half dozen blocks at home by cutting out the decks and profiles and penciling a center line around the block. Let the kids take it from here on with good, sharp jackknives and some supervision.

Best whittling award is bestowed to: _____

The _____ ship's model was created by _____

The _____ ship's model was created by _____

The _____ ship's model was created by _____

When the models are finished, tow them from the stern of the boat and "race" them. See which models do best in different weather and at different speeds.

Tug of War

This is a great game to play in shallow water with the tender, a strong swimmer, and a youngster who can row. Weave the painter under the thwarts of the tender and out the aft scull hole. Harness the painter under one of the swimmer's armpits, around the back of his or her neck, and under the other armpit. Then secure the end of the painter to the running part of the painter about two feet from the swimmer's back. Stand on the painter between the swimmer and the rower to guarantee that both children start working at the same time. Who is always the winner, regardless of power? Why is this so? Tug of war played on the beach is also lots of fun.

Man Overboard

Throw a round life ring overboard, and, with a youngster at the helm and another on deck with a boat hook, time how long it takes them to retrieve the life ring. On a sailboat, jibe as soon as the ring has been thrown, bringing the boat leeward of its previous course. On a powerboat, first steer away from the ring, so that it does not get caught in the propellers. Shift into neutral, or better, turn off the motor so that you can clearly see the ring. Circle slowly toward the ring, and get close enough only to reach the ring with the boat hook.

Best time   Record holder

Night Sky Watching

The best time to view the sky is near new moon, when you can see more than 2500 stars with the naked eye on a clear night. Star gazing is best away from city lights, which, along with a full moon, diminish the number of stars we can see to around 200. Observing the changing shape of the moon each night can be fascinating. After midnight in mid-August is one of the best times to see "shooting stars," or meteors.

Looking to the north, many people can locate the Big Dipper, visible year round although some of its stars will fall below the horizon south of San Francisco or Norfolk, VA. The Big Dipper, known to some as the Drinking Gourd, is a starting point for night sky watching. Four stars form the bowl of the Dipper and three stars shape the handle.

From the two pointer stars in the bowl of the Big Dipper, follow a line up to Polaris, the North Star. Polaris is not a particularly bright star, but it is always directly over the North Pole. You will know you have found Polaris if the star is at the top of the handle of the Little Dipper. Imagine a line from the top inner star in the bowl of the Big Dipper up through Polaris. Look past Polaris, and you come to the middle M-shaped constellation Cassiopeia, The Queen.

Look back at the Big Dipper again. Follow the arc that curves from the last star in the Dipper's handle to the bright star, Arcturus. Arcturus forms the point of an ice cream cone shaped constellation called Boötes.

Now look high in the south to the two stars, Deneb and Vega which can be found in line with Arcturus. Vega is very bright. Deneb and Vega form the base of the Summer Triangle, and Altair completes the triangle.

The star in the bottom right corner of the bowl of the Big Dipper is Merak. Follow a line from Merak to Arcturus and on to Antares, a large, bright reddish star. Antares is in the center of Scorpius, a scorpion-shaped constellation.

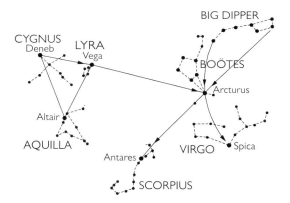

From late October to May, look to the south to find Orion. Three bright stars form Orion's belt. The star on the right in the belt rises due east and sets due west. Draw a line up through Orion's belt and you will see the red star Aldebaran. Looking up further you see a group of stars known as Pleiades, or Seven Sisters. Imagine a line from Orion's belt in the opposite direction, and you find the bluish Sirius, the brightest star in the sky after our sun. Sirius is at the neck of the Big Dog.

61

Knots to Know

All sailors should know the following knots at the minimum: bowline, two half hitches, clove hitch, square knot, and sheet bend. But there are literally thousands of knots, and the best sailors know the right knot, bend, or hitch for the right purpose. Record here your progress at learning these useful classics. For added challenge, try tying the knots blindfolded. Kids love to learn knots too.

Knots in the end of a rope:
Overhand _____ Bowline _____ Running bowline _____
Bowline on a bight _____ French bowline _____ Sheepshank _____
Blackwall hitch _____ Figure 8 _____ Cat's paw _____

Knots for bending two ropes, or for bending two ends of the same rope together:
Square knot _____ Two bowlines _____ Single and double sheet or becket bend _____ Single and double carrick bend _____
Reeving line bend _____

Knots for tying a line to a ring or spar:
Fisherman's bend _____ Timber hitch _____ Timber and half hitch _____
Two half hitches _____ Round turn and two half hitches _____ Clove hitch _____
Rolling hitch _____ Studding sail tack bend _____ Studding sail halyard bend _____

Splicing and whipping are two more techniques a proper marlinspike sailor knows. Worming, parceling, and serving protect rope from wearing and chafing. These skills have less use today when most rope is made of either nylon, polyester, or various high-tech fibers, but knowledge of these skills is useful, especially in fancywork.

Seagoing Library

Favorite books on seamanship are:

_____

_____

_____

Favorite sea adventure stories are:

_____

_____

_____

Suggested reading on board and during the winter:

Chapman's Piloting and Small Boat Handling, 6th edition
Annapolis Book of Seamanship by John Rousmaniere
Shipshape: The Art of Sailboat Maintenance by Ferenc Maté
Your Boat's Electrical System by Conrad Miller
Morrow's Book of Knots
Arts of the Sailor by Garrett Smith
The Onboard Medical Handbook by Paul Gill Jr., M.D.
Passport to World Band Radio
Find the Constellations by H. A. Rey
*The Compleat Cruiser: The Art, Practice and Enjoyment
   of Boating* by L. Francis Herreshoff
Sailing Alone Around the World by Captain Joshua Slocum
Peking Battles by Irving Johnson
Shackleton's Boat Journey by F. A. Worsley
Ice, Yarn and Other Sea Stories by Tristan Jones
Maiden Voyage by Tania Aebi and Bernadette Brennan
Adrift by Steven Callahan
My Old Man and The Sea by David and Daniel Hayes
The Bounty Trilogy by Charles Nordhoff and James Hall
Hornblower Saga by C. S. Forester
The Aubrey-Maturin novels by Patrick O'Brian
Swallows and Amazons series by Arthur Ransome

Illustration Credits

All illustrations are copyright Mystic Seaport Museum, Inc. (MSM) except where noted.

Page 6: Oil sketch {Ketch-rigged catboat} Milton Jewett Burns (1975.399). Page 11: Photograph detail {Shipwrights installing planking} (1986.7.1). Page 12: Photograph {Hickman sea sled underway} (1975.273.92). Page 13: Photograph {Sailing in the Mystic River} Newbury (1980.41.137). Page 14: Photograph {Oyster sloop *Nellie*}. Page 15: Photograph {*Elysea*}. Page 18: Photograph {Rigging detail, *Regina M.*}. Page 19: Photograph {Stern detail}. Page 21: Photograph {Walworth wrench display} Lawley Collection (1982.8.103). Page 23: Photographic Postcard {Spectators watching sail race} Wilma D. Fowler Collection (1989.69.67). Page 37: Watercolor *Cat Cay 6 March 1958*, James McBey (1967.256). Page 41: Watercolor {French Navy caricatures} H. Gervèse (1953.2931.4). Page 43: Photograph {Children playing on beach} (1985.18.26). Page 52: Postcard {Lighthouse, Marblehead, Ohio} (1994.37.197). Page 55: Photograph {Eva Collins Grinnell} (1983.57.183). Page 56: Photograph {Lawley & Son Boatyard} (1982.8.34) Lawley Collection. Page 62: Photograph {Knotboard detail} (1955.594). Page 63: Photograph {Shipboard library}.

Photographs from the Rosenfeld Collection at Mystic Seaport Museum appear on pages 4, 5 (above right), 8, 16, 17, 25, 26, 27, 29, 31, 32, 35, 36, 39, 42, 45, 47, 54, 57, and 59.

The following illustrations are copyright U. S. Coast Guard Museum. Page 5: (bottom left) Photograph {Cape Hatteras Light} (L5 45). Page 51: Oil *Minot's Light*, W. F. Halsall (996.043). Page 53: Photograph {Diamond Head Light, Hawaii} (L5 52). Page 58: Wood block {Children before schooner} (994.1184).

The star charts on pages 60 and 61 are copyright Scotch Bonnet Press. They were drawn by Rebecca Lehmann-Sprouse with thanks to Don Treworgy, Mystic Seaport.